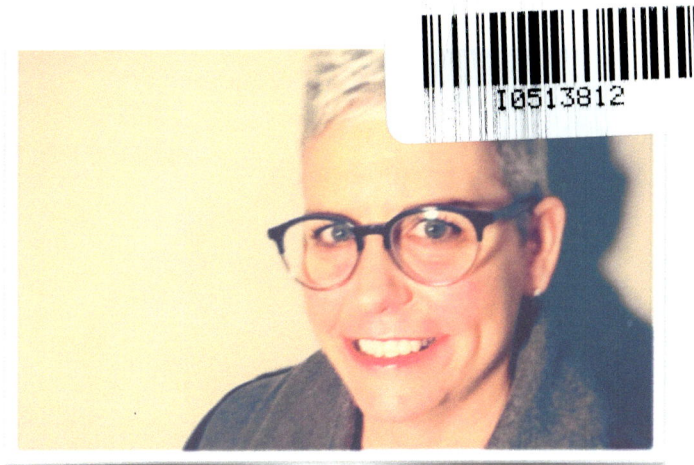

Loving Mystery: An Invitation

My paintings and poetry are the expressions that flow from meditation and reading spiritual texts.

For me, contemplative practice is an invitation to connect with the Divine.

In practice, I attempt to let go of thoughts and concerns, repressed emotions, fear, and unhealed grief. I experience waves of light, love, and healing images of my home in the Kentucky woods. The practice leads me to explore and express my truest nature, what is left as I let go of regrets and concerns. I begin to sense what has always been. While reading poetry and spiritual texts, the four words Sister Ilia Delio uses to describe the Divine help to synthesize fragments into an image or words into a poem. These words are; creative, evolving, expanding, and entangled.

The process can start while I am meditating, reading, writing, or simply with the act of putting paint on the canvas.

I am not an expert in any one of these.

The willingness to trust the practice is always the beginning.

This is the invitation.

Glory

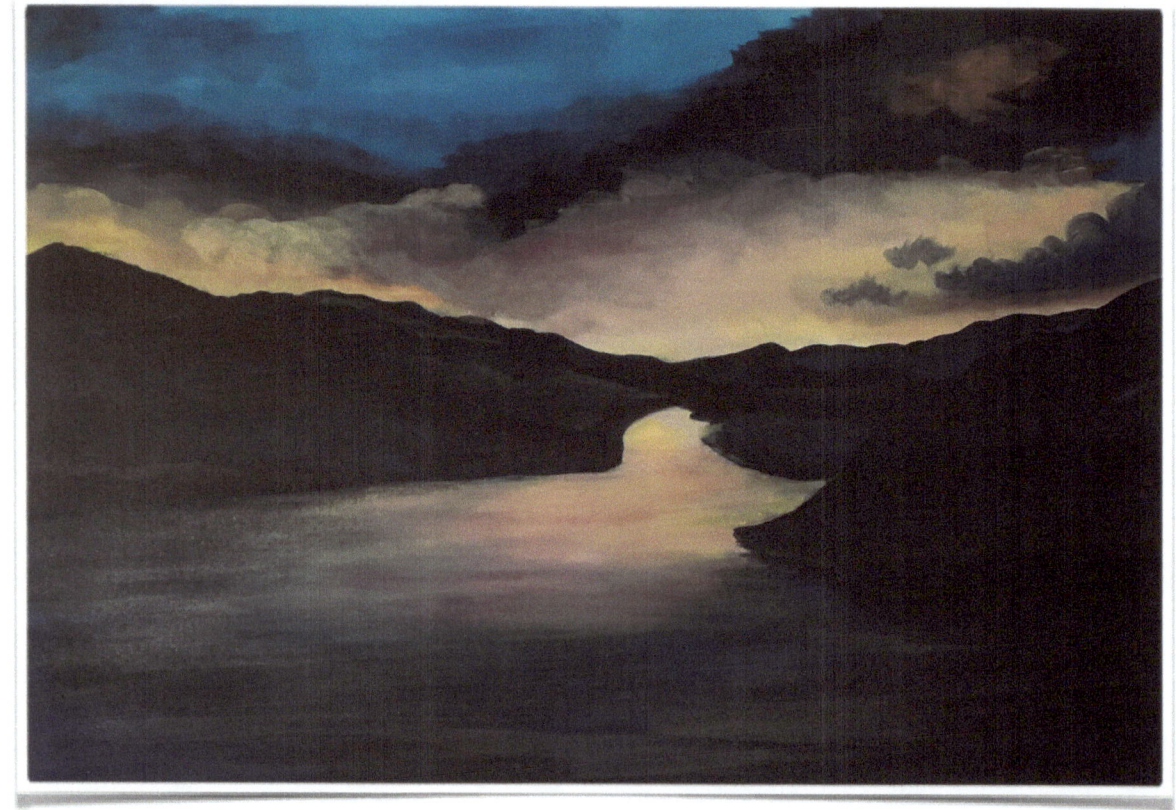

Brooke Summers-Perry   Summers-Perry.com

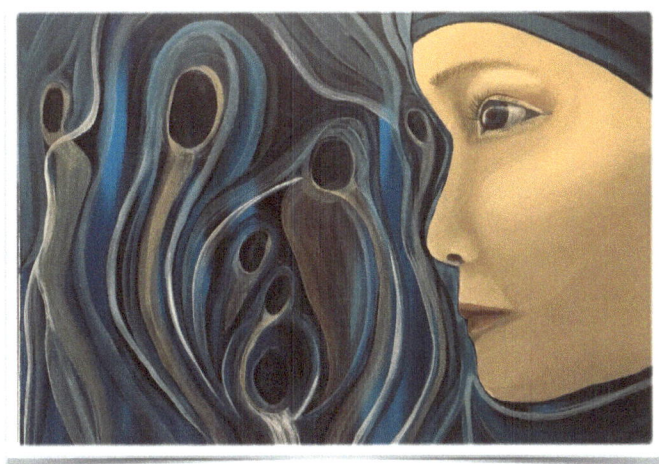

Moment 1/25/13

Rewrite of Psalm 131

It is only when I do your work that pride has no meaning for me.

My eyes rest on the present moment, only on what exists in your presence to be found in this moment.

Things that seem to be important in our world are shallow, meaningless, and melt away.

I release the grasp of the brass ring, the empty promises of our culture, and my heart is fully at peace.

I love and am loved and I rest my body and its longings. Your glory is waiting for me to let go and become still so it can be revealed.

Within me you live and move and breathe.

Allow my peace and connection with you be a way for others to see your grace.

Let me not be tempted to turn away from this knowing and being.

Dynamics

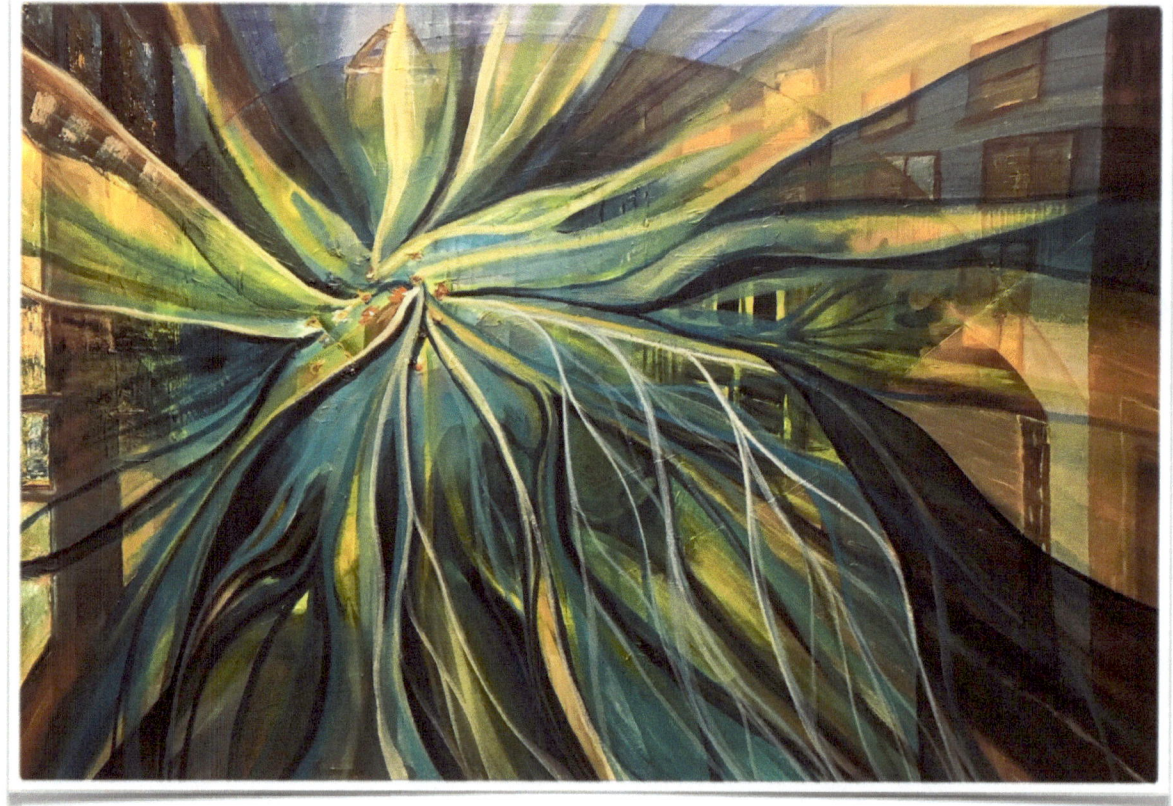

Brooke Summers-Perry

Summers-Perry.com

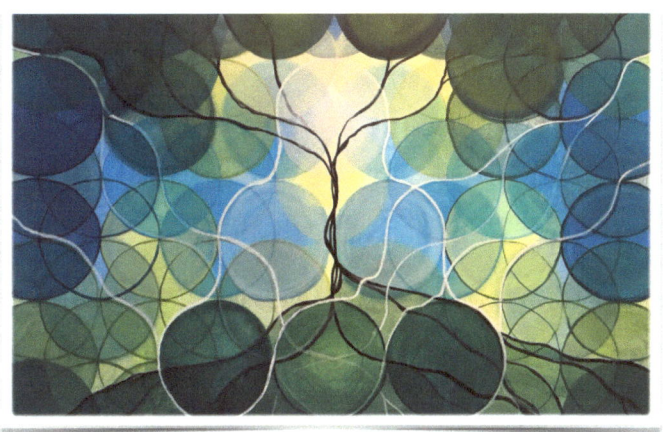

Release 10/26/14

We must free ourselves from our;
judgments,
limitations,
regrets,
patterns,
habits,
assumptions,
thoughts,
wounds,
resentments,
fears,
expectations,
and shame.

The more of these we release,
the more space we make for grace and peace.

Brooke Summers-Perry Summers-Perry.com

Clear

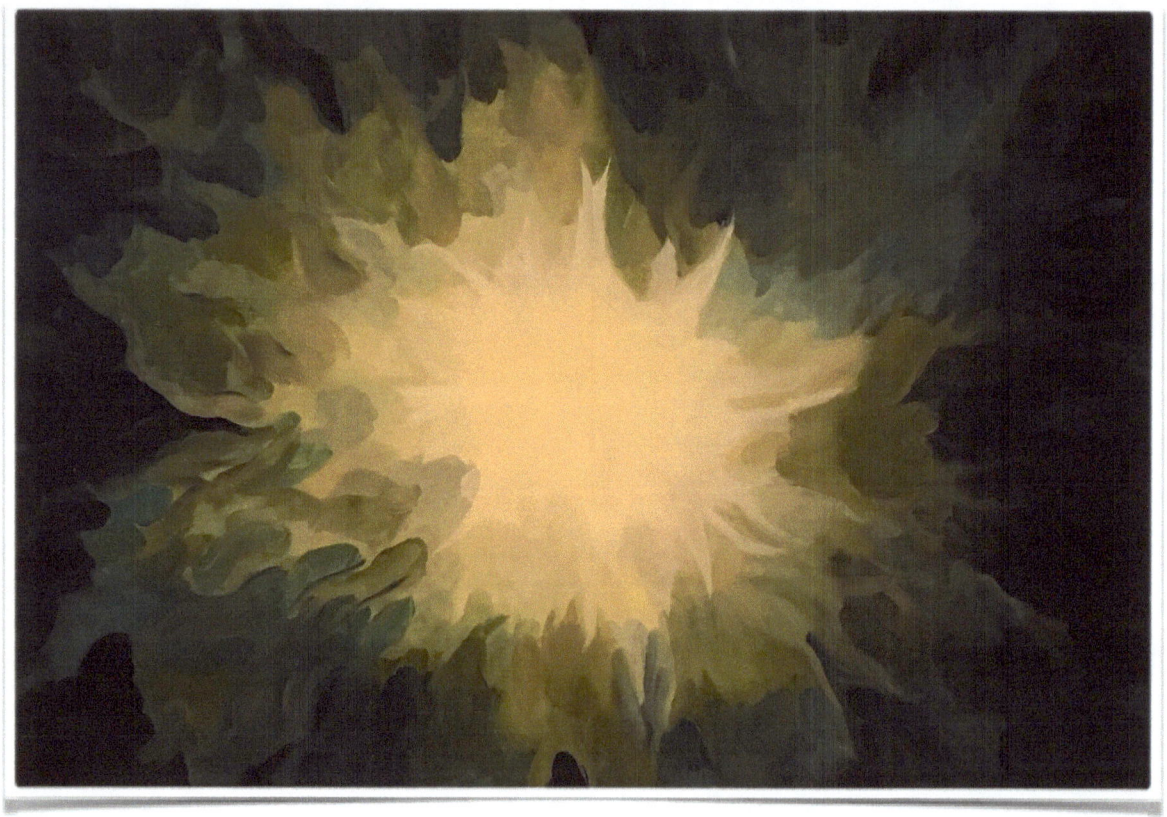

Brooke Summers-Perry

summers-perry.com

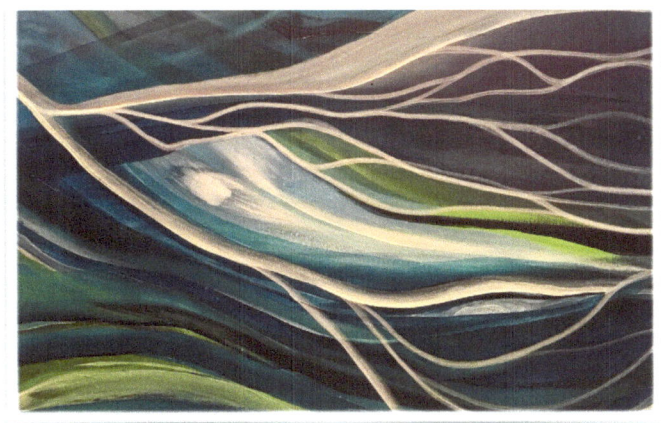

Stream Dance 6/15/15

Reflections of light stream through narrow windows. The shadows of branches and leaves dance with the shadow of a bird in flight. As we walk poised to refresh, renew, and restore, the world and love in all things dance around us revealing the dance we seek at every turn.

We are light, shadow, and the dance.

Eclipse

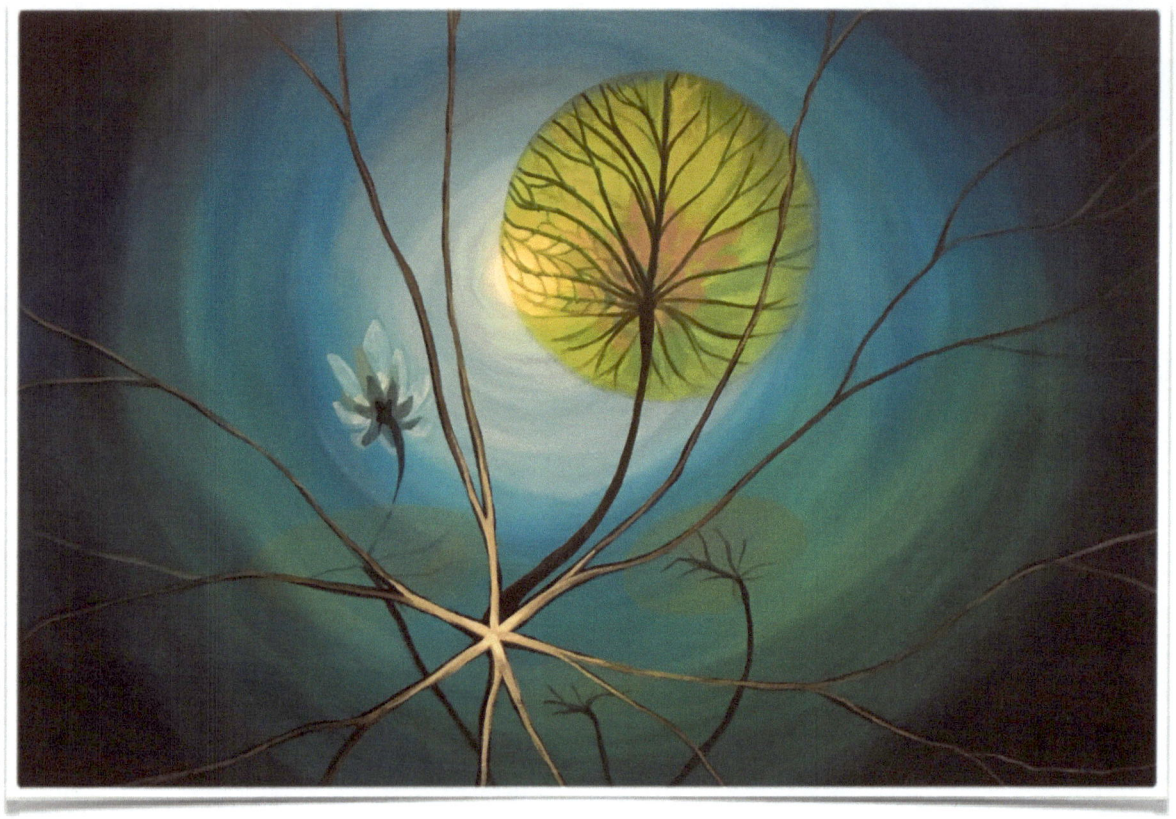

Brooke Summers-Perry

Summers-Perry.com

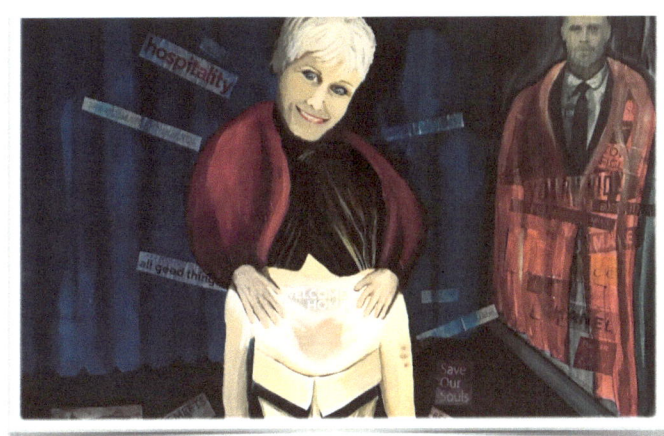

Return _{1/26/17}

Do not complain
Rather
Come plain

Come to the present moment without
comparison, expectation
or inordinate attachment.

Do not miss the merciful gift that is present in;
the breath
the light
the ground
the companion

When you wake, when you listen
when you come
they are here
as they are for every one.

Setting

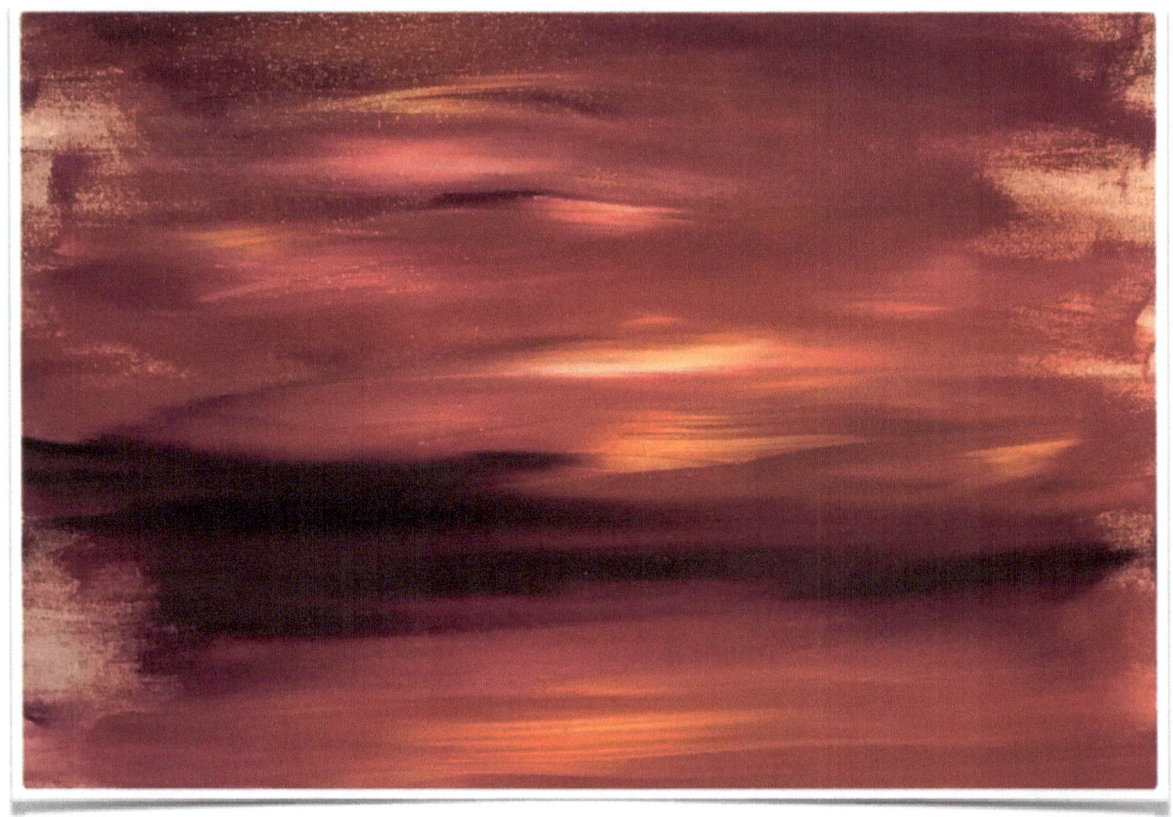

Brooke Summers-Perry · Summers-Perry.com

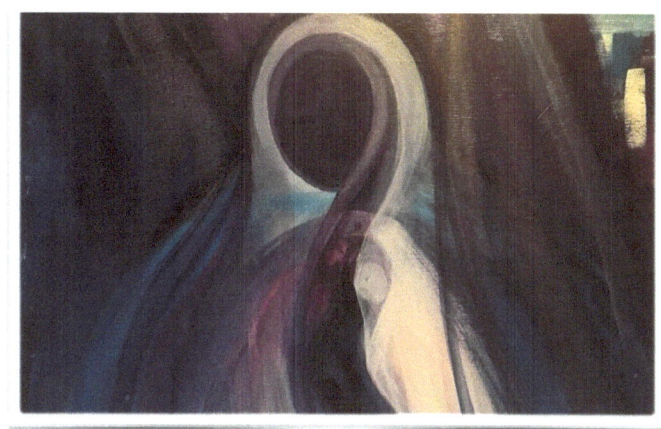

I See You 1/27/17

When all the light escapes me
and I no longer occupy
space here,
what I want to be remembered for is
the light I saw in you.

I see your light.

My heart smiles with yours.
Nothing else I've done here
matters any more than that.

Boat

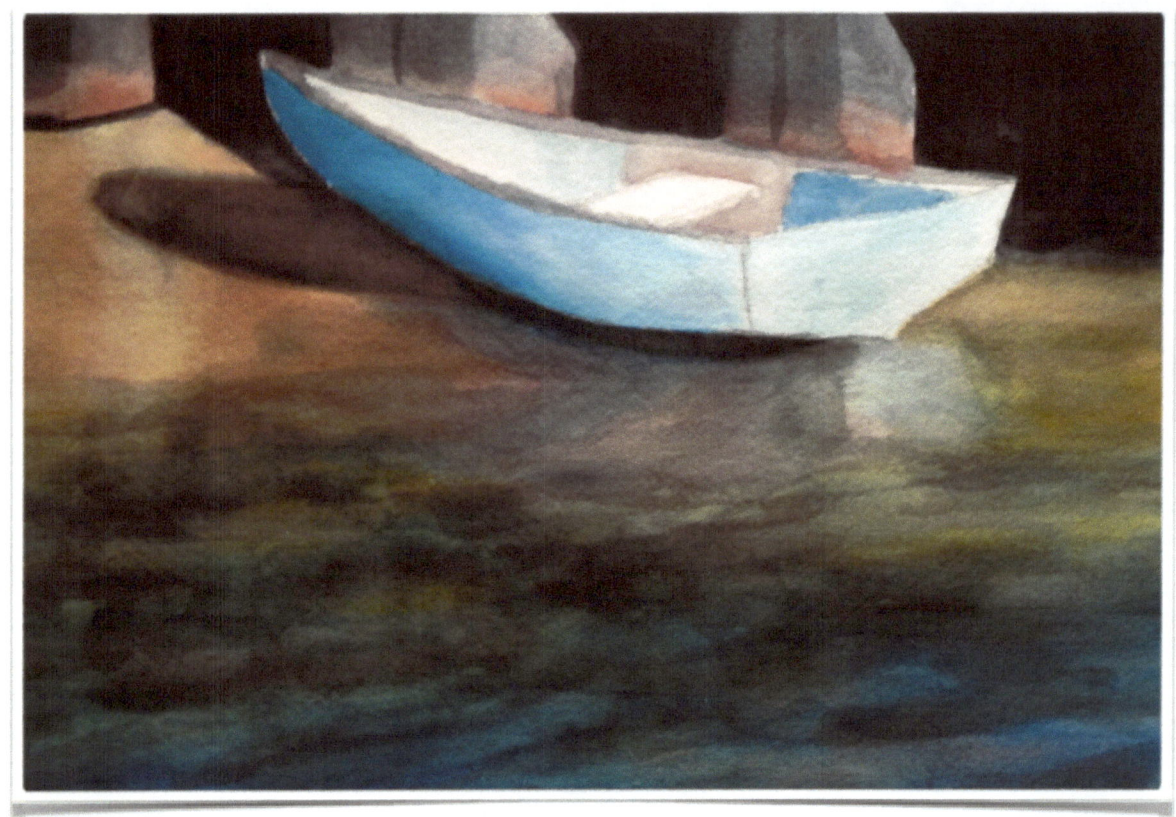

Brooke Summers-Perry

Summers-Perry.com

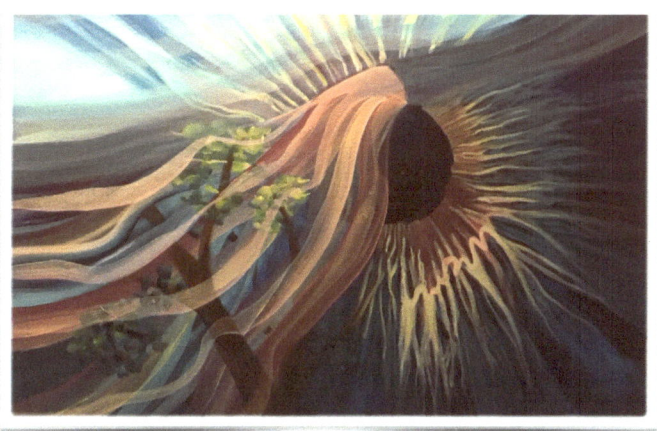

Work Through Me 2/19/17

Eyes that see
Burdens set free
Love work through me

Carriage

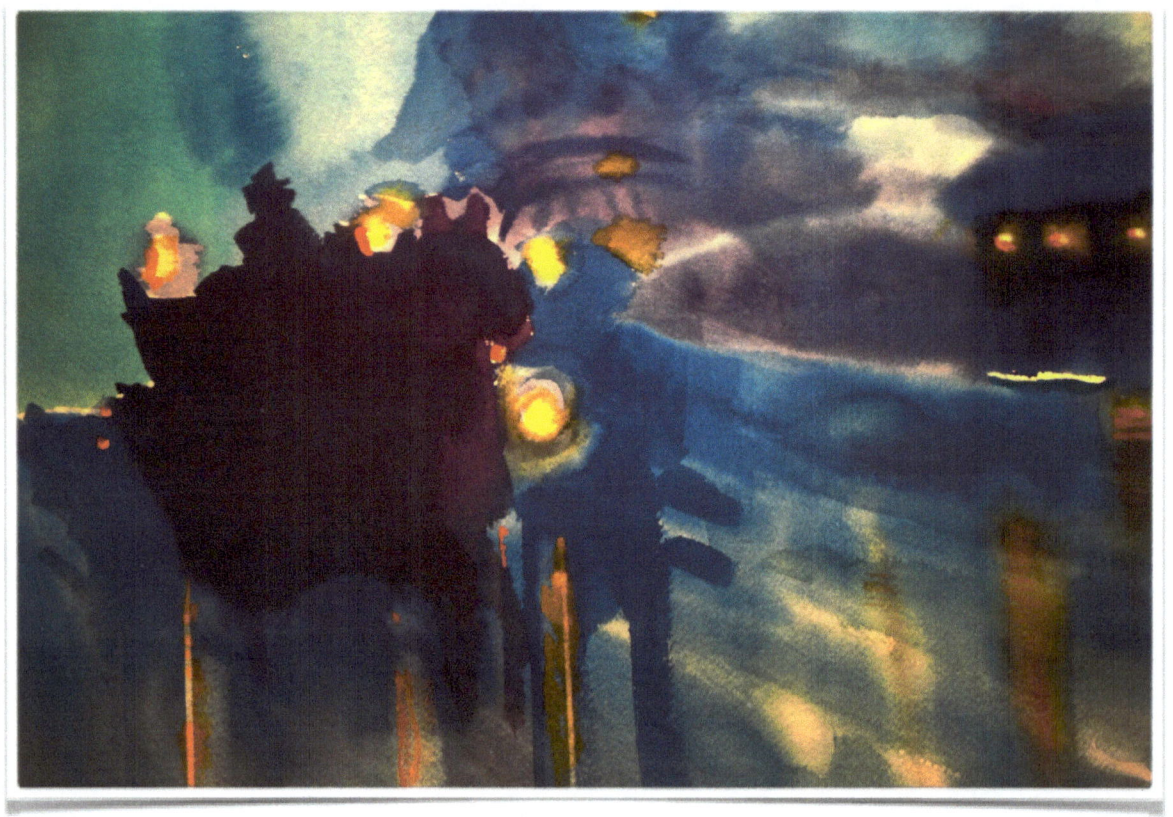

Brooke Summers-Perry　　　　　　　　　　　　　　　　　　　　Summers-Perry.com

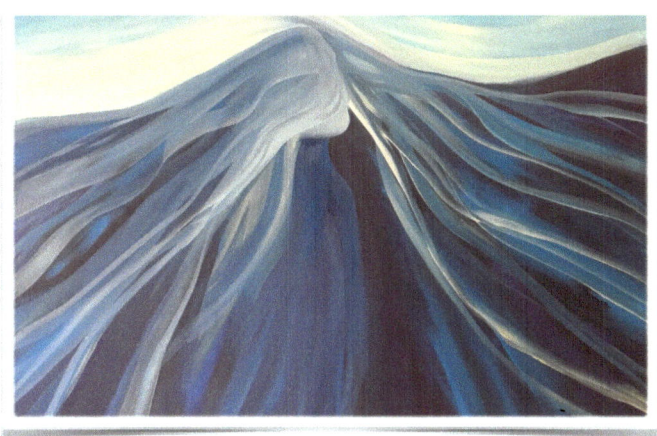

I Sit With Pain 3/29/17

a 4 yr old's protest
a collection of
every dismissed
feeling

a son's realization
that changes
carefully cultivated
friendships

a teen's
inability
to see the point
of any of it

I survive the pain

I sit still long enough
for the pain to catch up

I sit still enough to
know the mystery
of love within

I resist the urge to
make it my tantrum
make it my acceptance
make it my depression

I say just enough

go ahead
kick and scream
but not at me

go ahead
grieve the loss of
who your friends want you
to be

go ahead
mourn the absence of
the light you cannot see

you do not choose these
they choose you

ignored pain magnifies
ask me how I know

I meet you in the moment
I do not diminish
I do not cower
I do not take it from you
I do not live through it for you

I focus on my love for you
I focus on my faith in you

we do not
deny
distract
dismiss

I witness
I hold
I breathe
I love
I stand under
I sit beside

I watch you fall
tears and tissues cascade

last rush of grief releases

shoulders drop
belly softens

a grief finally released

a smaller self
destroyed

I watch you rise

Brooke Summers-Perry   summers-Perry.com

Succulent

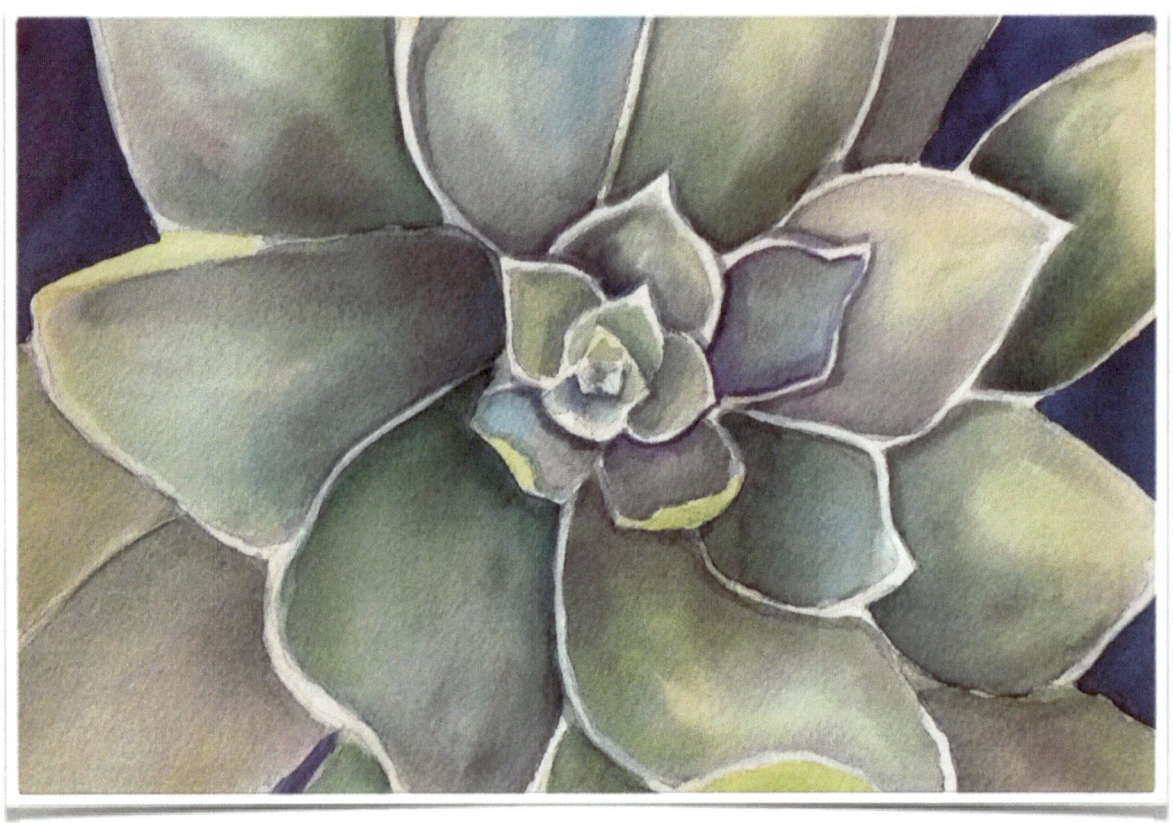

Brooke Summers-Perry · Summers-Perry.com

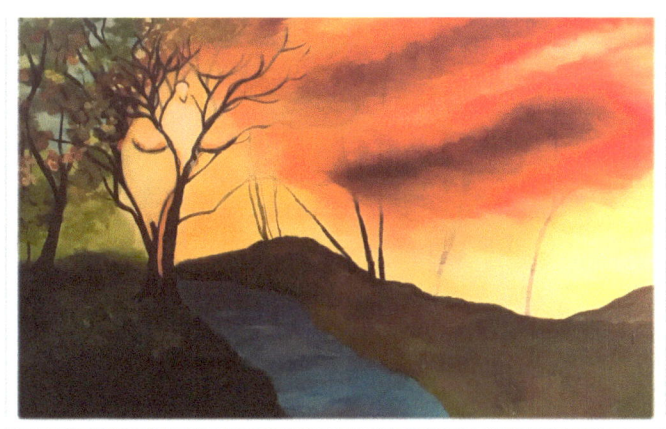

Finding Myself 8/6/17

You will find me
gently moving
deep in the wilderness
most quietly assimilating
refracting and bubbling
moving along with
the never ending cycle.
I am in process
returning back
to big expanses of water
collections of particles
unknowingly waiting
to transform and ascend
gather and descend
in showers of
solids or liquids
joining and nourishing
every living thing on the planet.
I am the current, the drop
the wave and the sea
I am the vapor, the sprinkle,
the rain and the storm
I am the smallest brook in the most remote wood
combining and changing
churning and returning

Seam

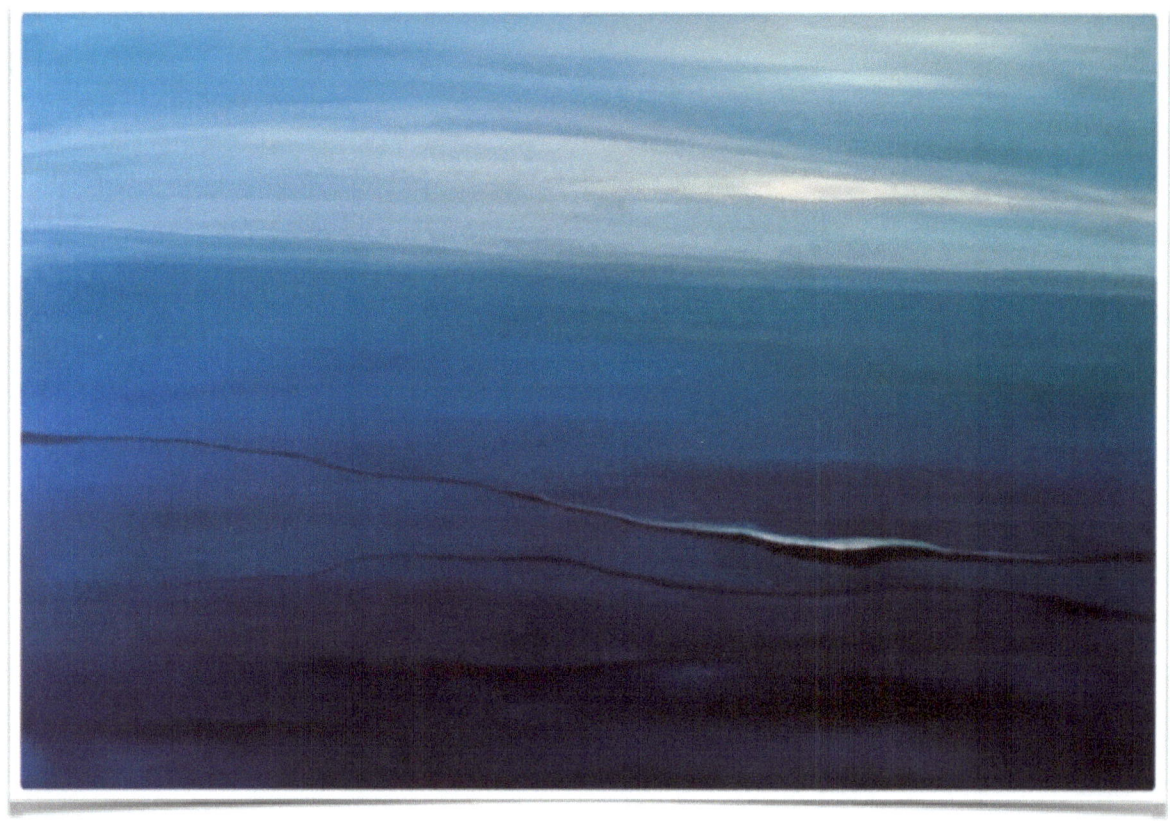

Brooke Summers-Perry

Summers-Perry.com

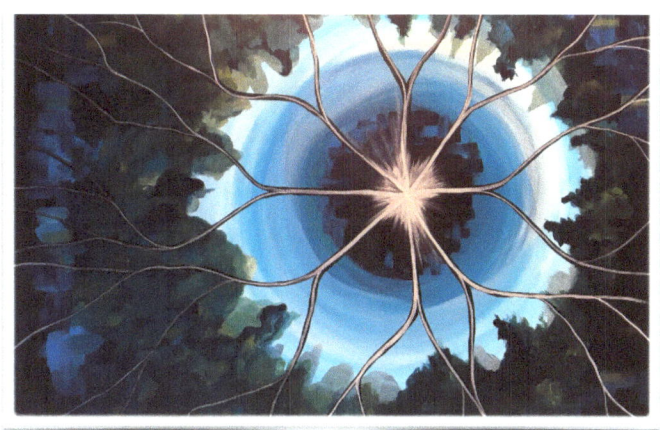

Harvey 9/15/17

As the barriers fail our myopic eyes
As the walls of loss build curbs yards high
As our lost heroes new wings dry
As the lifted veil reveals our cry
In the rising we wake
In the wake we rise

Layered

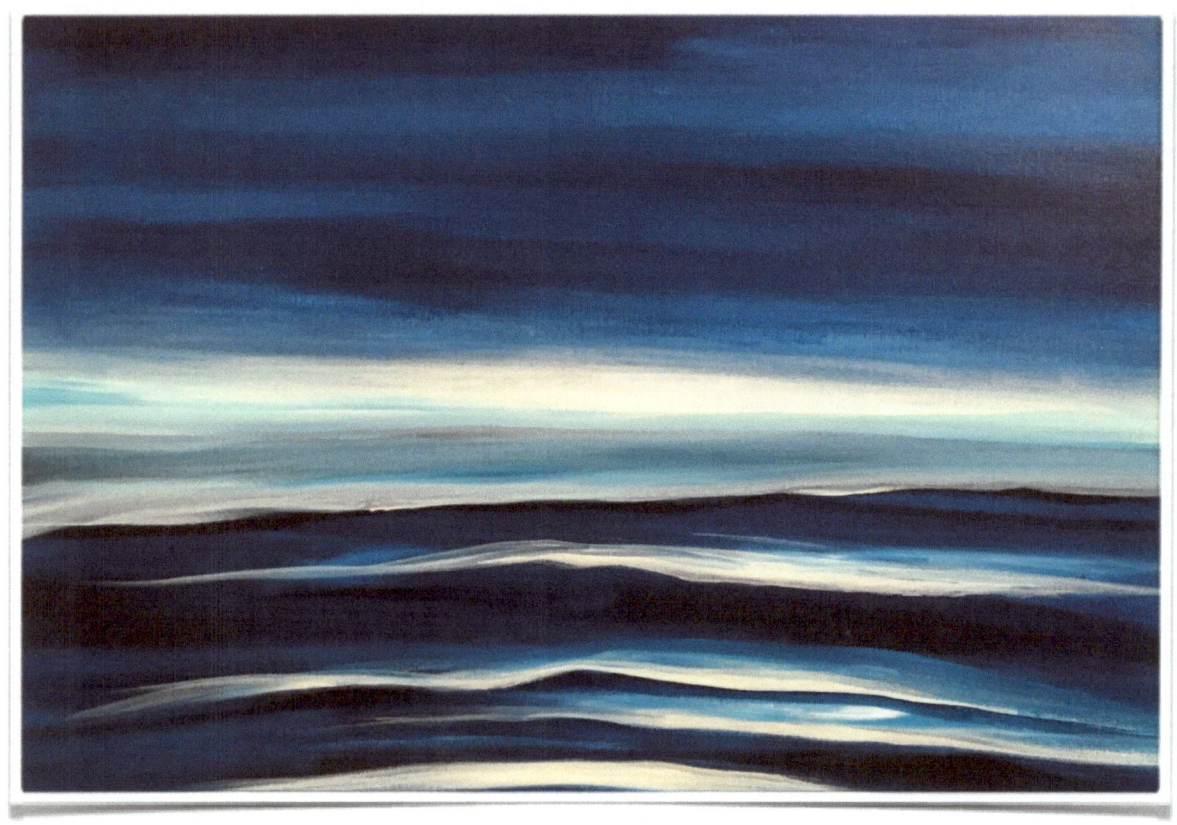

Brooke Summers-Perry   Summers-Perry.com

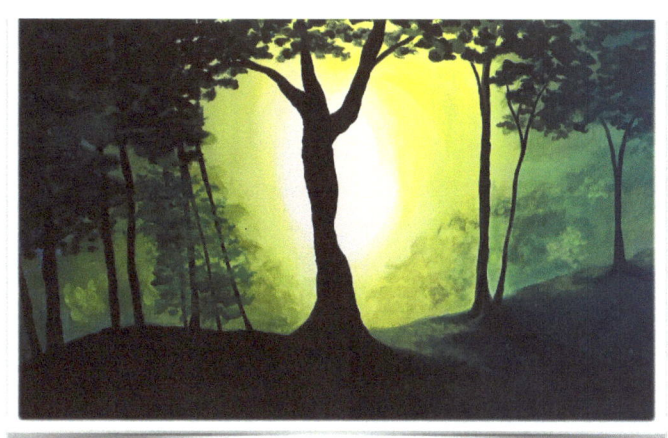

Expand _{9/19/17}

If fear calls you to
spread your roots
If loss births new branches to
fill the canopy
If anger clears the dormant
fibers of your trunk
If sadness leans you slightly to
rest on your neighbor
Then may you be
spread
filled
cleared
swayed
For you are far more
evolving
expansive
creative
and entangled
than the shell your seed can bear

Orchid

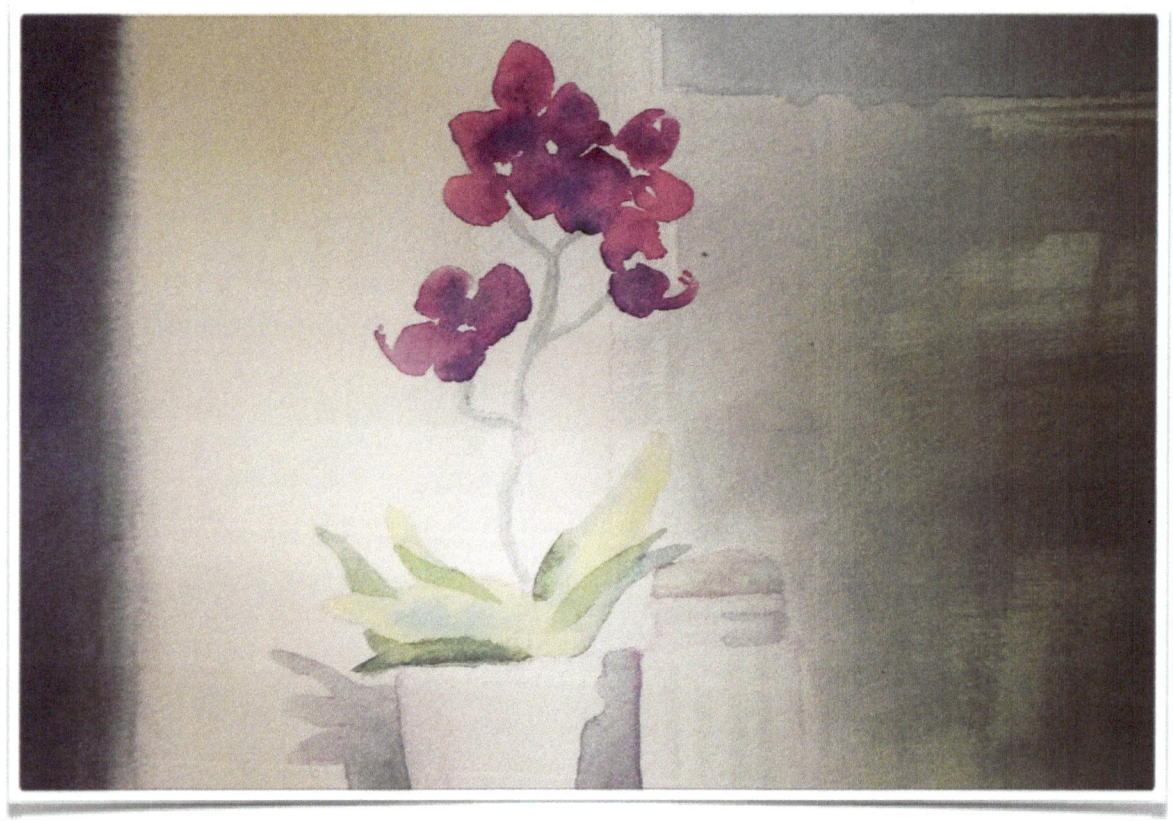

Brooke Summers-Perry   Summers-Perry.com

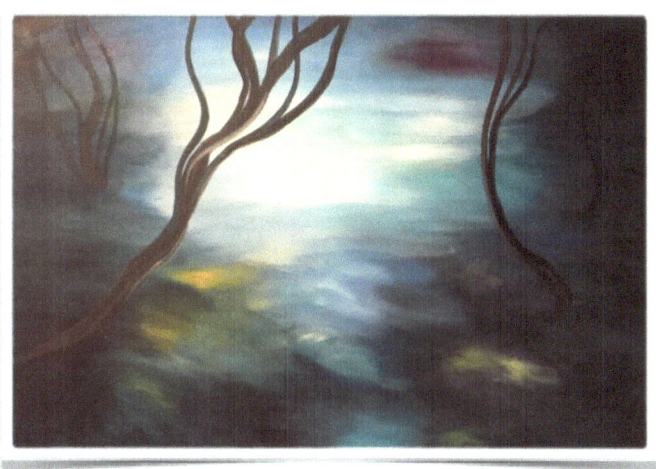

Enter 10/13/17

The Mighty Woolper, "Woolpert" if you are my grandfather, is what we call the tributary that meanders at the base of the foothills of the Ohio River. It carries crawdads, catfish, and cranky teenage girls in canoes. It harbors water moccasins, brownish foam, and snapping turtles. It runs in loopy zigzags adjacent to a winding road that bears its name. Connecting the road and creek is a 1/4 mile paved path that was first worn down by migrating snapping turtles.

This is the drive I traversed after my first date. The uneven rutted terrain is what I scarcely saw through a dance of leaf silhouettes filtering moonlight. I travelled the path alone on foot in order to save the undercarriage of a Camaro.

It was the site of a head on dirt bike collision, the exclamation point at the end of two oncoming sentences made up only of a sibling's name at full volume and terror.

It is the manifestation of leaving the stage and entering the play.
It is the gateway to God's country.
It is the path that holds me to a turtle's pace.
It is the way to my happy place.

Practice

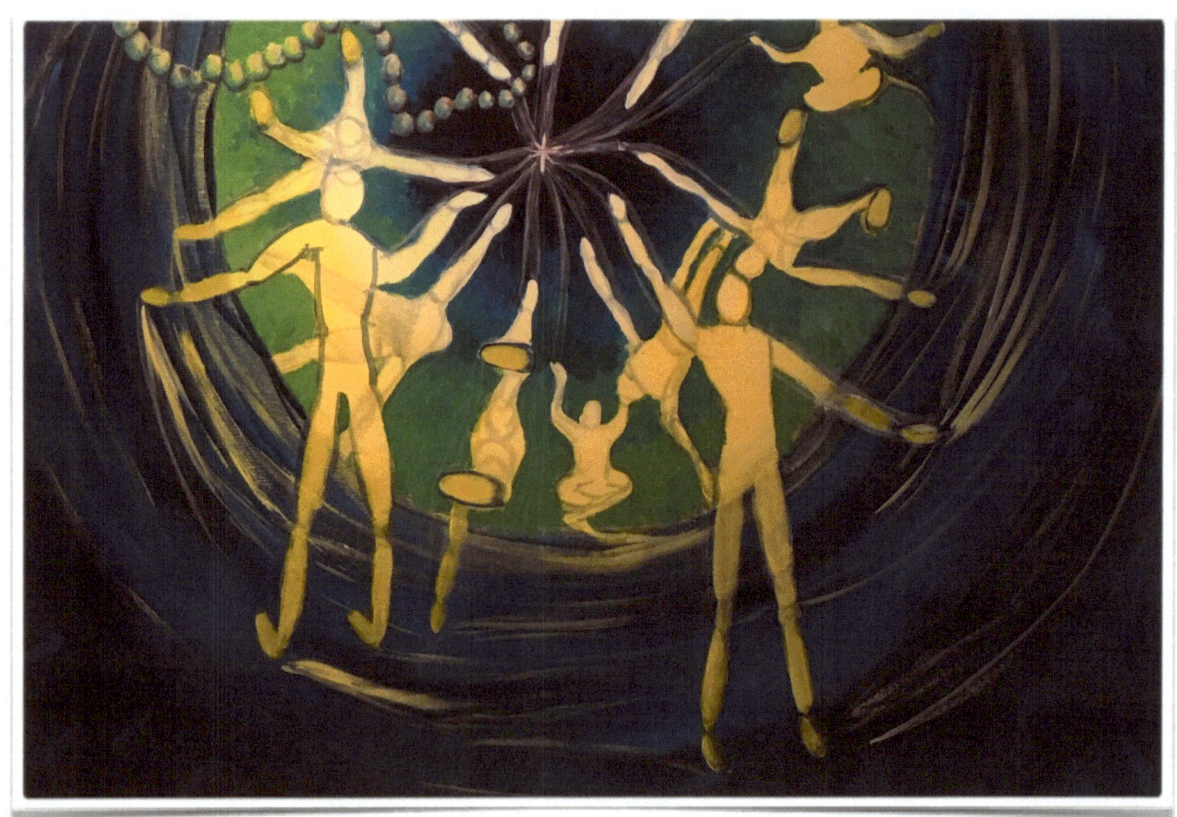

Brooke Summers-Perry

Summers-Perry.com